Stefan Glowacz · Uli Wiesmeier

ROCKS
around the world

translated by
Martin Boysen

SIERRA CLUB BOOKS · SAN FRANCISCO

Translators Note: The activity of "Sport Climbing" referred to in this text is what English-speaking climbers call hard free climbing, that is high standard rock-climbing without recourse to artificial aid. Free climbing is a comparatively new phenomenon in West Germany where the focus of attention until recently has always been the high mountain faces of the Alps. Routes on these faces, with their length and objective danger, tend to sport aid points wherever the climbing becomes difficult. Speed of ascent is the main consideration and consequently no one worried too much about how the routes were climbed. Unfortunately the crags and *klettergarten* were treated like diminutive mountains where the same semi-artificial grab-and-pull techniques could be practised as training for the real thing.

In the early seventies the ideal of "clean climbing" was imported from the United States by a few zealots who had made the Yosemite pilgrimage. They set about cleansing their own crags, eliminating superfluous aid points and tackling the climbs in a totally free manner according to the new ethic. Not everyone appreciated it, and for a period undeclared war raged between these brash "sport climbers" and the traditionalists. Since then the popularity of free climbing has increased enormously, such that it is now grudgingly accepted by the old guard.

As this book acknowledges, free climbing has been going on in one form or another in many countries for a long time. Indeed in

Note for 1996 edition: Since 1988 Germany has reunified into a single political entity; however, the two schools of climbing remain distinct, with East German sandstone retaining its tough ethical codes, which are widely respected.

Britain, with typical insularity, we like to think that we invented it, although the East Germans have an equal if not stronger claim.

In Britain (on free climbs) pegs were largely rejected with the exception of the odd aid move on the hardest climbs, whilst in America pitons and the occasional bolt were the accepted form of *protection* but were scrupulously avoided for aid. The British used slings, chockstones and (from the early sixties) nuts for protection. By the late sixties nuts were being used by leading climbers in the United States but it was not until the early seventies, when they were improved and marketed by the Chouinard company, that they came into general use. The combination of nut protection and American ethics made clean climbing possible and this initially found its greatest expression in Yosemite Valley.

When introduced to mainland Europe, clean climbing rapidly developed its own set of rules with French attitudes to the fore. Bolts have been important in opening up the huge limestone faces of southern France. Pre-preparation and top-roping, intensive training not to mention a touch of exhibitionism are all part of the present scene. Not surprisingly standards are ferociously high and getting higher! This book, written by one of the very top practitioners and illustrated by a leading photographer, provides a valuable record of this varied world of rock-climbing in the late eighties.

MARTIN BOYSEN Manchester 1988

The Sierra Club, founded in 1892 by John Muir, has devoted itself to the study and protection of the earth's scenic and ecological resources – mountains, wetlands, woodlands, wild shores and rivers, deserts and plains. The publishing program of the Sierra Club offers books to the public as a nonprofit educational service in the hope that they may enlarge the public's understanding of the Club's basic concerns. The point of view expressed in each book, however, does not necessarily represent that of the Club. The Sierra Club has some sixty chapters coast to coast, in Canada, Hawaii, and Alaska. For information about how you may participate in its program to preserve wilderness and the quality of life, please address inquiries to Sierra Club, 730 Polk Street, San Francisco, CA 94109.

Copyright © 1988 by Rosenheimer Verlagshaus

Sierra Club Books paperback edition: 1996

First published by Rosenheimer Verlagshaus, Rosenheim, West Germany

Library of Congress Cataloguing-in-Publication Data

Clowacz, Stefan, 1965-
    Rocks around the world.

    1. Rock climbing.   I. Wiesmeier, Uli   II. Title.
GV200.2.G59 1989   796.5'223   88-11406
ISBN 0-87156-885-3

Printed in Spain
10 9 8 7 6 5 4 3 2 1
D.L. B-25.276-88

INTRODUCTION

The idea of a photographic climbing odyssey around the world came to us four years ago in Verdon as our spirits were warmed by the sun of southern France. We wanted to produce a book which captured both the fascination of climbing and the beauty of the climbing environment.

It is a book produced by two rock-climbing fanatics who have travelled to four continents to fulfill their aim. What we offer here represents thousands of miles of air travel, thousands of rope lengths and countless rolls of film. This is the state of the art of rock-climbing in the late eighties.

We rejected locations that were merely exotic and sought out areas that had a history of climbing and from the start resolved not to produce a climbing travel guide. Instead we have concentrated on creating an impression of each area rather than a catalogue of factual information. This may not be to everyone's taste but it is what we wish – it is our personal statement.

So – climb on board, chocks away, fasten your seat belts, hold on, the journey is about to begin!

STEFAN GLOWACZ and ULI WIESMEIER
Bavaria, Germany 1988

F R A N C E

The readership of climbing magazines rises; whole school classes go to the crags; autoknackers (car thieves) enjoy the high season in Verdon; the walls become a stadium – climbing is a branch of show business. In France climbing is idolised.

France has everything a climber could desire. It's a cornucopia of climbing

enough to satisfy the appetite of the most hungry enthusiast. It has been so for a long time.

Since the start of "Sport Climbing" this is where the standards have been set, where trends have been initiated, unhindered by the stultifying rules and regulations of old conservative climbing clubs and officialdom. Climbing is accepted as a sport much like any other, rather than an adventure for the crazy few – a satisfactory state of affairs for both professionals and amateurs.

Where else are there so many films on TV concerning climbing? Where else are the best climbers household names? With such a huge following it is hardly surprising that there are so many extremely able climbers and that France is a forcing ground for new developments and ever-rising standards.

Geographically, France is blessed with a perfect combination of rock and climate. If you were to climb there all year and every year you would never run out of outstanding routes because there are so many different areas to visit and so many climbs to do.

For example the Verdon Gorge, in the heart of Provence, offers 300m walls of rock of a quality unsurpassed anywhere in the world. Whilst the kayaks weave and bob down the torrents far below, and tourists creep on all fours to the canyon edge to take in the awesome view, climbers hurl their ropes over the belvederes to descend to their routes – for there are few climbs which start from the bottom. Should you take your camera you are likely to get some impressive photos. If you don't it will very likely be stolen from your car!

To have eyes only for the rock would be considered ignorant in France. Moonlight, lavender fields, old abbeys and intimate villages, red wine, fresh baguettes and the chirruping of cicadas are all part of the charm of the scene. You break off some fresh bread, accompanied by one of the hundred or so available cheeses; you brush off the crumbs from your lap and consider where to climb next. Perhaps Buoux, 100km north of Aix?

Here the limestone is hard, and eroded by water into incredibly abrasive and painfully sharp holds. It enjoys great popularity particularly in autumn, winter and spring. Easter and Whitsun are the busiest periods, so much so that it has led to the valley being closed to climbers. Proper sanitary arrangements became an absolute necessity, and rubbish had begun to accumulate below the cliffs. Here too the light-fingered operate successfully! Whilst the climbers wrestle to unlock the cruces the thieves have an easy time solving their own technical problems!

Thinking of combinations, in nearby Monaco it is best to view the Casino only from outside – in particular from the crags – that is until we have the earning potential of the local tax-exile tennis stars! The view from the many splendid routes

down onto the millionaires' playground is truly impressive.

You don't have to go to the South to find rock: in the middle of France just outside Fontainbleau is a bouldering paradise. Innumerable sandstone boulders up to 30ft high provide absorbing problems for soloing. At weekends the whole of Paris seems to head for the rocks. Entire families scramble and slide around the circuits. You are quite likely to stumble into a fashion show with professional photographers clicking away at models prancing through the boulders, while brilliantly bedecked climbers flit around like hummingbirds, totally absorbed in their own beauty of movement.

In France it is possible to live comfortably as a professional climber, and even if in this commercial merry-go-round sychophantic adulation does cause a few climbers to become arrogant, most remain comparatively unspoiled. The climbing is nevertheless gloriously simple – a sport to be enjoyed, uninhibited by rules, regulations or profound philosophies.

Yesterday perhaps a helicopter-assisted assault of the three north faces; today a route climbed blindfold – anything goes! The French are always good for a surprise – the event is everything. The show must go on!

Gorges du Verdon

You break off a chunk of fresh bread to eat with
one of the many cheeses, you brush the crumbs
from your lap and wonder – what next?

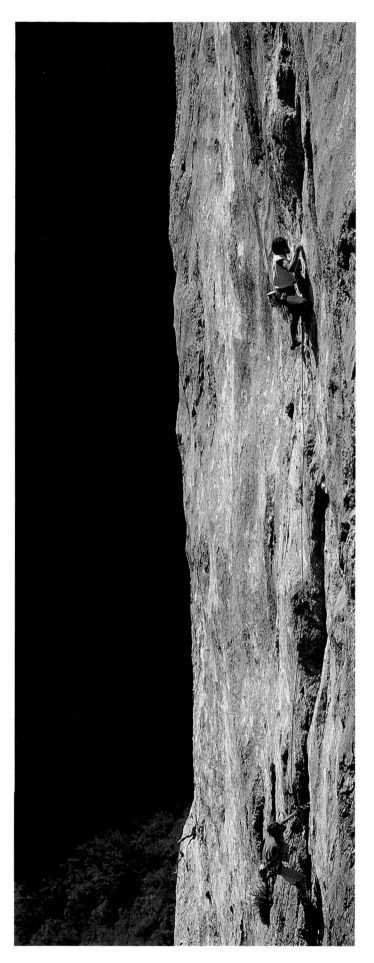

Liqueur de Coco, 7 c +
Verdon

Mijo, 8a
Verdon

11

Papi on Sight, 7c +
Verdon

Debiloff, 6c +
Verdon

Emballéz c'est pesé, 8a
Verdon

Sector *Frimes et Châtiments*
Verdon

Papi on Sight, 7 c +
Verdon

Take it or Leave it, 8 a
Verdon

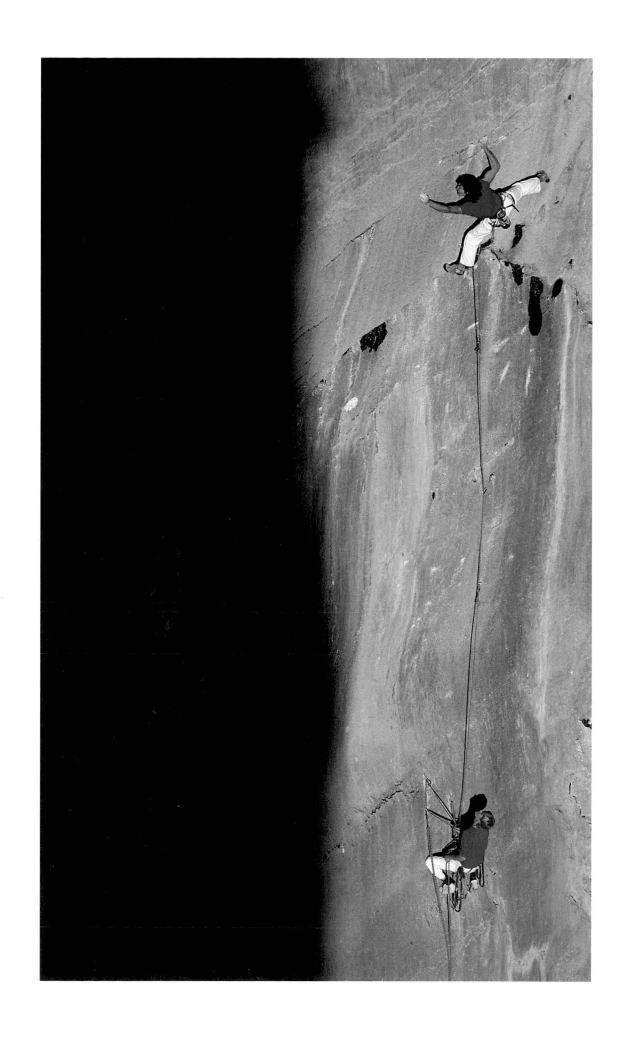

Rêve de Papillon, 8a
Buoux

Rêve de Papillon

La Rose et le Vampir, 8b
Buoux

La Rose et le Vampir

Orange Mécanique, 8a
Cimaï

Orange Mécanique

En un Combat Douteux, 8a
Cimaï

Samizdat, 8a
Cimaï

E N G L A N D

It all pointed to a clear starlit night; a gentle breeze and hardly a cloud to be seen. It was so still and lovely that we wanted to sleep out under the open sky. It was taking a chance, but surely tonight it wasn't going to rain. At about two in the morning, thoroughly drenched, we erected our tent. It was pouring with rain. Welcome to England.

I already knew from experience that in England one of the worst risks is that of the weather. I also knew that the climbing is not to be compared with that of France. But I was sufficiently intrigued by its long history and traditions to return once more. On my first visit I had concentrated entirely on climbing the hard routes but now I was equally interested in meeting climbers, to learn more about their approach to the sport. From my researches I had established that England has as long a history of free-climbing as the USA*.

Despite the proximity of England, free-climbing attitudes came to the continent from across the Atlantic rather than from across the Channel. By the early seventies, as a reaction against the damage caused by excessive pegging, the clean-climbing ethic was born in the United States based on the use of nuts for protection.

Although this type of climbing is bound up with the philosophy of leaving the rock untouched, the continental imitators have largely substituted the use of nuts with bolts, and these have often been placed liberally without regard to the climbing environment. The crackless nature of some of the best European cliffs makes bolt protection essential, but climbers have made little effort to restrict their use to a reasonable minimum.

This overprotected European style has led to the rapid emergence of a particular type of new route which when re-exported back to the US, led to a split in attitudes – one group wishing to protect the old philosophy of "clean climbing" while another was happy to adopt the new European trends. My view is that the overprotection of routes robs climbing of one of its main ingredients – the psyche, fear, or the atmosphere of adventure.

During lengthy evening discussions in the pubs I began to warm to the ideas of the Brits, not to mention the beer. In Britain bolts are now increasingly being used and many top climbers are worried that this is going to undermine the traditionally adventurous style of British climbing. They maintain that while bolts cannot be ignored

in the development of the sport they should be used sparingly, to prevent serious injury or death. In the British view ability should not be measured solely by athletic prowess. The most highly regarded climbers are those who combine great athleticism with steadiness and judgement in a stressful situation.

This demanding ethic seems initially rather daunting – almost a "put-off" to discourage participation, but it is an important consideration. Twice climbing development has gone up a blind alley. One such aberration was the era of the Direttissima when all that was needed was a plumbline and a vast stack of bolts. Fortunately this soon lost its charm. The reaction to this was free-climbing – more demanding, more fun, and following the natural lines of weakness. But the new freedom was soon corrupted by over-use and abuse of protection. Climbing was reduced to a circus act performed a few feet above an ever-present safety net. This type of climbing also soon begins to pall and is another blind alley. To escape from it we have to examine the essential elements of the sport.

We have established that with the help of artificial aids it is possible to climb anything but this totally defeats the basic idea of climbing – the use of hand- and foot-holds to gain height. Moreover excessive protection also corrupts climbing by removing the element of uncertainty and creative personal judgement. When it comes to consideration of free-climbing and the nature of risk, soloing springs to mind as this combines physical and mental abilities.

In Britain climbing has evolved according to its own traditions; new trends are not automatically adopted. Here there are many difficult routes that have little or no natural protection and no bolts and have, in effect, to be soloed. In Germany, Italy and France many climbers have turned to soloing as the answer to the otherwise monotonous safety of the climbs, to recapture the element of freedom and risk.

Thank God there are no rules or official arbiters of risk to tell us what we can do! Everyone is responsible to himself. Certainly the risk stakes are rising – routes of the highest possible grades are being soloed. At this rarified level any mistake can have fatal consequences. This deadly dance of death can be dangerously seductive – offering a buzz impossible to achieve in any other way. A well-known climber told me that he has experienced his most intense feeling after such an ascent and found he discovered the joy and beauty of life afresh. I only hope he does not mix up his freedom with free fall.

Soloing at this level is not for me and I am happy to climb without constant fear of death. I do appreciate a degree of danger however, and the rush of adrenalin at the possibility of a fifty foot fall is intoxicating. This is a stimulation I can't do without.

* See translator's note on page 4.

Revelations, E6/6c
Peak District

London Wall, E5/6a
Peak District

Edge Lane, E5/5c
Peak District

Luckily there are no officials
with clip boards to dictate rules.
Everyone is responsible to themselves.

Strawberries, E6/6b on sight
Tremadog, North Wales

Left Wall, E2/5c
Llanberis Pass, North Wales

Right Wall, E5/6a
Llanberis Pass

Left Wall, E 2/5 c
Llanberis Pass

Cool Diamonds, E4/6b
Cornwall

Isis, E4/6a
Cornwall

Isis, E4/6a
Cornwall
_____

W. Greinwald: *Isis*
M. Edwards: *Lunatic Owo*, E6/6c
Cornwall

Titanic, E6/6c
Cornwall

U S A

We wanted to cross a desert.

Four thousand feet of granite, merciless sun, temperatures up to 100 degrees in the shade, as if there were any shade! It was a crazy idea that had become fixed in my brain. The desert is a wall, *the* Big Wall, and this is no exaggeration. By the time I realised this it was already

too late. The dream had already turned to a nightmare. But it's easy to be wise after the event.

Extreme climbing today is no longer confined to small crags. The great challenges are to do totally free ascents of some of the famous Yosemite big walls. I recall my last stay in the Valley with mixed feelings. I had invested my entire stock of nervous energy and motivation into a free ascent of the Salathé Wall. I had gambled for big stakes, and I had lost. Perhaps it should have remained a dream.

It was difficult enough to get detailed information about the route. Opinions varied. Some thought a section rated 5.11, others thought the same pitches would be impossible. I became more confused with every new enquiry. I didn't want our project to fail because of some minor oversight, but what could we do? In the final

analysis we would have to trust our own experience and hope that we would be fully prepared. We traced each pitch minutely on the topo. We double-checked our equipment and borrowed a few necessities.

Days passed. Again and again we drove through the meadows directly below the mighty wall of El Capitan to size ourselves up against the imminent challenge. Our topo seemed hopelessly inadequate in the face of the reality of this endless granite. The closer we got the smaller we felt and our self-confidence dwindled correspondingly. When I saw pictures of the big wall, I felt respect for it, but now I felt nothing but awe.

Of crucial importance was the problem of food and drink, which would have to be sufficient to last our four-man team for four days with a small safety-margin. It's easy to sit below in the comfort of a hamburger joint trying to calculate what you will need in extreme situations. If you forget anything it's too late, McDonalds haven't yet opened a Salathé Wall branch.

Another worry was the heat that was expected in early June. We had been warned about this, and the severe dehydration it can cause, and we were fearful about running out of water at a

critical stage of the ascent.

I lay awake at night, unable to sleep, tormented by doubts which had been suppressed in our daytime discussions. Now I felt vulnerable and had to keep morale up by telling myself 'Stefan, y'ur gonna beat that wall, man.'

At five in the morning I was exhausted with nervous tension, but finally I managed to snatch a couple of hours sleep before it was time to get up. Uli and I had wanted to start early because we knew several other teams had designs on the route. We climbed the first third of the wall and left fixed ropes. By the afternoon we were at the pendulum pitch to the Hollow Flake and I made preparations for climbing this section free by inserting two protection bolts. Then we abseiled back down the ropes.

One more night in camp; this time I felt calmer and had a good night's sleep. At 5am the next morning we went back up to the wall, this time

accompanied by Harald and Bennie to help us haul the heavy sacks – two 90lb monsters. So this is what big-wall climbing is all about! But they had to be carried because they contained all our extra water supplies, and with great difficulty we dragged and hauled them up the route to our advance base on the Mammoth Terraces. Climbing, pulling, climbing, pulling, hauling – we worked until we were totally exhausted. No chance of making any more progress today, the sacks were far too heavy. The weight had to be reduced. It was untypically cool for June so we decided we could leave half of the water behind. We deposited our haul bags and abseiled off for one more night in the fleshpots.

On the next day I was actually looking forward to getting to grips with the unknown. And with every push of the jumars I was leaving civilisation behind. 'This is it, enough of the theory, now you have the chance to prove whether you are equal to this test.'

The first big hurdle, and certainly the most famous pitch, was the Hollow Flake which had never been climbed free, having always been overcome with a huge pendulum. My earlier preparation paid off and with the assurance of the protection bolts my attempt succeeded. I felt a keen sense of elation in being the first person to free this famous pitch. The climbing was very difficult and demanded total commitment from body and brain. A balancing act one thousand feet above the meadows, with the bolts providing a sense of security for a grand circus act. At the stance I needed no applause to know that I had won the first important round in this game, but there were still others to come before we reached our goal for the day – El Cap Spire. 'OK what's the next big pitch? The Double Crack. Fine I still feel strong for that.'

Hours passed like minutes. The climbing was strenuous but we coped with it. The stances were unnervingly small for four climbers and under these circumstances safety is not only a technical but also a psychological problem. The growing height was increasing the sense of tension among us. It makes no difference of course if you fall a hundred or a thousand feet, but my subconscious found this difficult to accept.

Now we were at the Double Crack. I took Uli's advice and tried to climb it quickly but to no avail. Soon the confidence gained on the Hollow Flake pitch drained away in the face of painful fist jams. The climbing became increasingly difficult and finally I was reduced to using old bolt holes, but they provided little support. I lost all coordination, time started to run out, I was cramping up and getting desperate. The sun was setting and we still had two pitches to go to the bivouac site. In desperation I tried to bypass the crack on the left, clawing up on tiny crystals but with no success. I couldn't believe it – to have to give up at this point, just halfway up the route. Dammit, nobody had warned us of this pitch. They had all talked about the Headwall. Was this to be the end – in Round 2? Deeply disappointed, I lowered off and Uli climbed the pitch using aid allowing me to climb it free but with a top rope. In this way we reached the bivouac platform. We

were now faced with a choice for the morning: we could either descend and try again to free lead the Double Crack, or we could carry on up the route and return later to attempt the pitch.

But now there was a new problem, that of the food. I had used up a huge amount of energy and was craving good food which we just didn't have. We checked our provisions carefully and it was clear that we had only just enough food to complete the climb. As I ate my meagre ration it was painfully obvious that we had seriously miscalculated the food aspect of the logistics. Most of our food was that typical American supermarket soggy junk food made of refined flour and I don't know what we were thinking about when we put these rations together.

My dream was slowly turning into a nightmare. We hadn't reckoned with meeting these problems. Months earlier when I was training I was obsessed with one thought, with every repetition of my punishing exercise routine I muttered to myself 'Salathé free'. And now I was burnt out, wrecked and drifting into sleep.

Next morning I soon realised that I had had it – I felt more and more tired. Even on the easier pitches my muscles weren't recovering and I was heading for a total breakdown. This happened on the fourth pitch – a holdless groove forced me to give up. Finally the wall had counted me out – KO in Round 3. There was no way around the problem and anyway all my motivation had gone. Even my companions had stopped urging me on, they were too concerned with their own problems.

The second bivouac proved to be the hardest

night of my life. My tiny food ration only made me hungrier, and sleep was impossible on the rock platform as my body craved relaxation. I was racked with cramps in my arms and legs.

The next day I had great difficulty in just following Uli and Harald up the fixed ropes on jumars and had to concentrate very hard to avoid making a mistake. I hated this granite, these merciless cracks, all I wanted was to escape from this rock desert that had so ruthlessly exposed my limitations.

As I said before – it's easy to be wise after the event. I am sure we were the first people to make a serious attempt to climb the Salathé free but I now realise that it was not serious enough. Those who try first often have to pay a high price for experience. But such a price? Arriving at the top I had no stomach for the grand panorama, I just wanted to get down to a good meal and a sleep, lots of sleep. Then I just wanted to slip away unnoticed from the scene of my humiliation.

Perhaps we were one generation too early for this mammoth task? Perhaps to climb the Salathé free requires a much larger order of organisation and support – a full scale expedition? This is not my scene, not yet anyway.

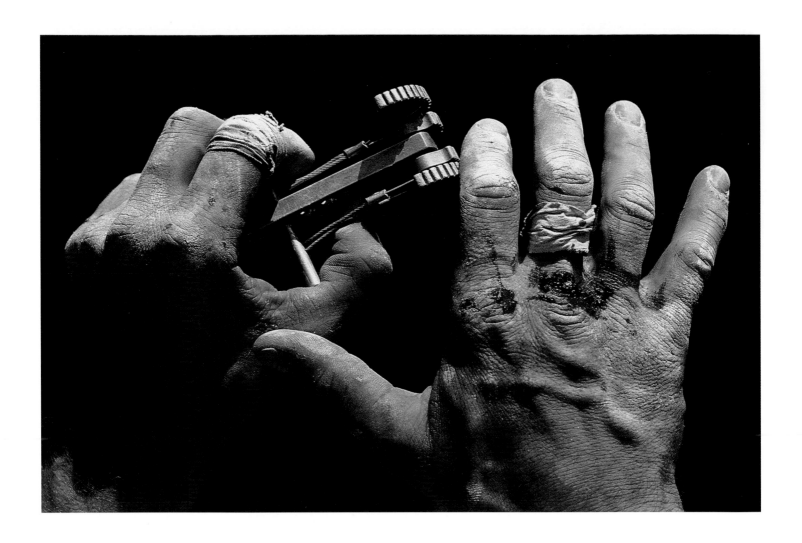

I hated this granite, these endless cracks.
I just wanted to get out, to escape from the rock
desert which had so cruelly exposed my weaknesses.

Alien, 5.12b
Yosemite Valley

Needles, California

Scirocco, 5.11d
Needles

Pyromania, 5.13b
Needles

Needles, California

Smith Rocks

Chain Reaction, 5.12c

Smith Rocks

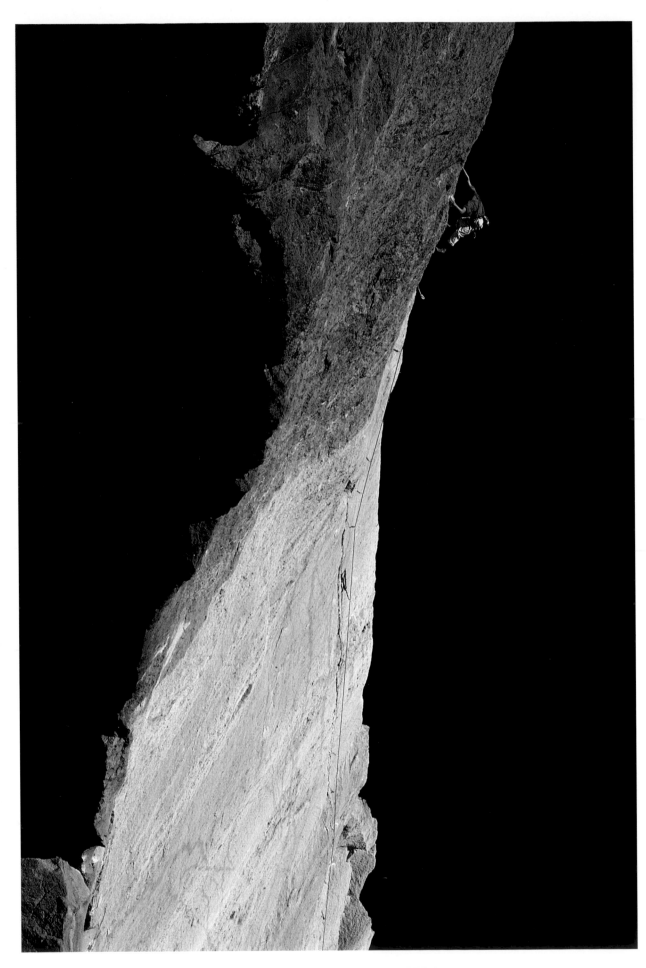

East Face of Monkey Face, 5.13d
Smith Rocks, Oregon

East Face of Monkey Face

Smith Rocks

Chain Reaction, 5.12b
Smith Rocks

Watts Tots, 5.12a
Smith Rocks

Rude Boys, 5.13c
Smith Rocks

Red Rocks, Nevada

Desert Gold, 5.13a (1st Asc.)
Red Rocks

J A P A N

Seije Hotchi belongs to the new generation of Japanese rock climbers – one of the best in his country – and he often accompanied us on routes, showed us around and became a good friend. Then when the holiday drew to an end we said 'Sayonara', and climbed into the plane hardly thinking we would meet again. But the climbing world is small: just six months

later I met Seije again in the campsite below Mt. Arapiles in Australia. There was a little colony of Japanese, a half dozen climbers encamped there for two or three months. They had come to test themselves against the routes. At breakfast, this time without the obligatory fish soup, we spoke together and I recalled my impressions of the land of the rising sun.

The first day began in total confusion. After the arrival at the airport we would have been lost without the friendly help of a local guide. We would probably have managed to get to the city centre by bus but we would never have found our way to any climbing areas. The signposts and traffic signs are entirely in Japanese characters – nothing for our western eyes to grasp and comprehend. All of a sudden we realised how helpless illiterates must feel.

It was quite an adventure for us to travel to the centre of Tokyo by train. Unsuspectingly we entered the carriage innocently thinking of our own homely subway. For the first couple of stations it wasn't too bad, but then the doors opened again and a tidal wave of human beings swept in. We were pinned in, trapped, and we could only hope that this crush of bodies would clear when we reached our destination. The idea of being enclosed for a couple of hours in such a sardine tin filled me with such horror that for some time I suffered nightmares about endless journeys on that teeming roller coaster of humanity.

After all this overcrowding we were naturally happy to leave the city for the sea and to get to grips with the cliffs of Jogasaki. Here, at last, we could give ourselves up to the pleasure of climbing.

'Rock-climbing is a comparatively new development in Japan,' explained Seije Hotchi. Japan has an alpine club of ninety years' standing, and Japanese climbers have tended to concentrate on mountaineering and alpinism, with particular emphasis on Himalayan activity and periodic adventures in the Alps. Rock-climbing has been totally neglected until the last few years. Slowly the good news filtered in from Europe and the

USA and the new trend was taken up. As with everything it does not take long for the Japanese to catch up.

At our destination we observed many young climbers thronging the bays of the mile-long cliffs.

'Despite the fact that the cities are a long way from the crags rock-climbing is getting ever more popular,' declared Seije. Even though people have to travel some 400km, lots of people go every weekend to the crags and mountains full of enthusiasm for their new hobby. I could see this for myself here at Jogasaki. A whole mob of climbers pointed out routes for me to do, watched me execute the moves and then demanded to know how they compared to international standards.

'Please climb that one,' they pleaded with friendly laughter as they hounded me from one

route to the next. I was not bothered about putting on a show. It was not a question of them sand-bagging me or trying to test me to my limits; it was just their pure enthusiasm which encouraged me.

'We are always delighted to have top climbers visit our land,' explained Seije, 'In this way we see for ourselves the best performers and gain inspiration to follow in the footsteps of Europe or America.'

Although Japan is bigger than West Germany it boasts only two really worthwhile climbing areas. After a couple of days we left Jogasaki and, passing by Mount Fuji, we travelled inland to Ogowayama. This is their most important climbing area, with a large number of hard routes. It is also a site of great natural beauty with granite crags rising out of huge birch forests. Our lodging place was typically Japanese: a wooden hut with partition walls of paper and hard rice-matted dormitories.

Satori, our host, despairingly tried every night to introduce me to the art of Japanese cooking, but our efforts collapsed early with unwashed rice which consequently stuck in a gelatinous mess.

Seije assured me that Ogowayama has countless opportunities for new routes. In contrast to the sea cliffs, where the rock is often moist if not wet, the rock here is a compact and sharp-edged granite. Another of the area's advantages is its size, giving plenty of scope for the coming wave of climbers.

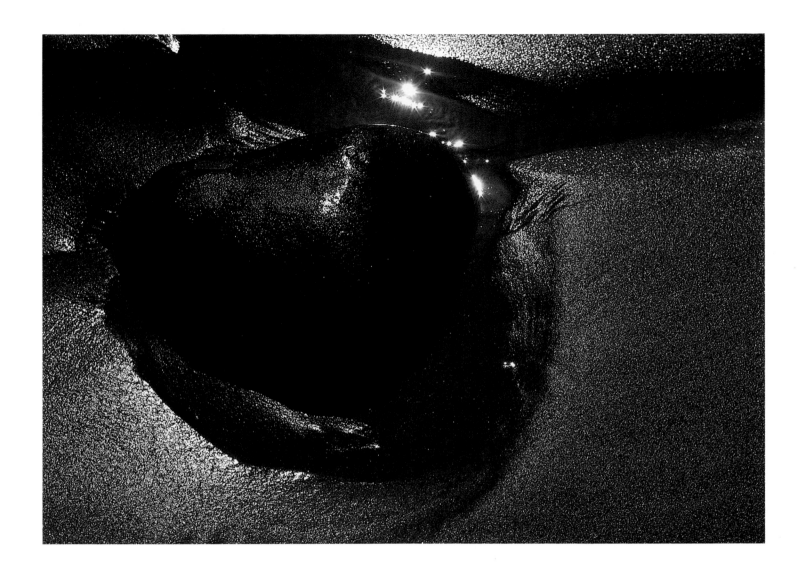

In contrast to other ancient traditions, rock-climbing
in Japan is comparatively young, though its
mountaineering tradition goes back 90 years.

Jogasaki

Circus, 5.12a on sight
Jogasaki

Circus

Colossus, 5.12c
Jogasaki
***
Jogasaki

Scrimps, 5.12c
Jogasaki

Ninja, 5.14a (1st Asc.)
Ogowayama

Super Injim, 5.12b on sight
Ogowayama

Fawcett Edge, 5.12c
Ogowayama

Isabelle Patissier: *Silk Road*, 5.12b
Ogowayama

Spider Line, 5.11b
Ogowayama

Spider Line

A U S T R A L I A

If only it was like I imagined it as a child, upside down and held in place by a weird force. Below me a 20 metre rock face and then nothing but the deepest Antipodean blue sky. All I have to do is effortlessly climb down overcoming the gentlest force of gravity, reach the edge of the cliff and then plunge into the cloudless sky as if it were a vast shim-

mering swimming pool. Childish dreams of the southern continent – down under in Australia.

My torn fingertips tell a different story of hanging on with my last ounce of effort to a tiny knife-edged hold. So climbing in Australia is just as hard as anywhere else – the top is still the top though, to be honest, I was feeling pretty down-under.

Mind you it had been a close thing. Everything had gone smoothly: a first ascent was almost in the bag – up until that vicious little fingerhold inflicted its minor injury on me. It would take at least two days for my finger to get well enough for another try. Why did it have to happen just now? The others have pushed off to Horsham to go swimming but I sit alone at the start of the route and rack my brains. I would like to call it "Lord of the Rings", but first I must climb it! It is this little problem which is gnawing away at me

and giving me no peace. A gently overhanging wall confronts me with a rating of 31/32 on the Australian scale of difficulty, which so far only goes to 32. Kim Carrigan, the foremost developer of Mt. Arapiles, has played on this problem for a couple of years. Naturally this spurs me on and yet at the same time it spoils my ability to relax and enjoy my surroundings fully. I feel as if I have mislaid a key and am unable to rest or think of anything else until I have found it. Two climbing days and two rest days I have invested in my route. I had to find the key to it – it just had to go.

I return to the campsite directly below the climbing area. Camping is free: there are no officious park rangers to wave rules and regulations on you, only the occasional slightly pompous fire warden checks up on our cooking arrangements. Fortunately the fires are swiftly extinguished by a tube of Fosters.

On weekdays there are usually more tents than climbers, and some tents are left standing for months. The absent occupants are usually dedicating themselves to wine – not drowning their sorrows at some climbing failure but picking grapes at Plantagen. It's a favourite casual job.

In the evenings we gather around a beat-up collection of car seats cannibalised from various wrecks, and cook over a small fire. The food tends to be already half-cooked by the sun. The food all comes from Mr Delaney's store, a favourite hang-out which provides everything a climber needs: magnesium, milkshakes, magazines and melons. In the evening sandwiches come free if they have remained unsold all day.

I feel greedy and would love to throw restraint to the wind and have a good blow out, but I must hold back a while. The locals are friendly and relaxed. They drift off to play darts and come back to the bar to down a cool beer and have a chat. We feel at home here.

Mind you I will only be able to unwind when I have finally solved the problem of "Lord of the Rings".

After the two restless rest days I am ready. I warm-up carefully and go through the route in my mind like an actor rehearsing his lines. I know each hold and sequence fluently. I cling to the wall like a fly on a window pane, but I am made to pay for a loss of concentration by falling off. I painstakingly mark out every false hold but even then I make a balls of it and come crashing down again.

Will my self-confidence survive this wall? I will soon know. At first everything goes to plan, I climb quickly and economically to the last dynamic sequence below the top. A fall then turns the serious attempt into one more general inspection. Once more I examine the last stumbling block – I will have no time to study it the next time around, the moves must be done without hesitation.

Another round, another renewed attack. After a long pause I throw my all at it and with every move my doubts diminish, I am calm and no longer nervous. This time nothing holds me back.

A first ascent. It's done and I suddenly feel overjoyed as I pull over the top wall and climb as if in a trance to the abseil chain.

The nervous tension, the doubts of the last few days fall away from me. I can let go at last – glide into the blue – even if it is only the local swimming pool at Horsham rather than the sky below!

Organ Pipes,
Mount Arapiles, Victoria

Punks in the Gym, 32 (2nd Asc.)
Mt. Arapiles

Punks in the Gym

Anxiety Neurosis, 26
Mt. Arapiles

Lord of the Rings, 31/32 (1st Asc.)
Mt. Arapiles

Eric Talmadge: *Lord of the Rings*
Mt. Arapiles

Watchtower Crack, 17
Mt. Arapiles

Bluffs, 18
Mt. Arapiles

Anxiety Neurosis, 26
Mt. Arapiles

Kachoong, 21
Mt. Arapiles

Upside down – a weird force keeps me
from falling. Under me a 60-foot rock wall
then nothing but blue sky

Dach ohne Namen
Mt. Arapiles

Anxiety Neurosis, 26
Mt. Arapiles

Mt. Arapiles

Climbing is an addictive drug from which there is no escape. Having once tasted it, one is driven on in crazy pursuit of the next fix; no matter the weather, no matter the hardships, only the next climb counts.

Mind you, I couldn't help reflecting as I wandered through the gloomy, dripping forest, given the choice I would rather have had a

nice sunny day. Even so, the bad weather had its compensations, the damp mists which wreathed the landscape gave it a sinister, fairy-tale quality. The bizzare shapes of the Elbsandstone towers stood outlined in the fog. Dark chasms disappeared up into grey nothingness. My eyes followed the line of a great pillar upwards and I relived the desperate struggle I had so recently experienced. I tried to pick out the line – yes, that's exactly the spot where, just two days ago, my life hung in the balance. I clung onto the rock and hung there – as precariously as the present line of drips – waiting to be stripped off by the first little squall.

The rock glimmered in a mottled patchwork of damp as the rain water trickled down following the line of least resistance. I couldn't help seeing a tenuous parallel with my own sport. The rainwater is subject to the same laws of nature, the same rock configuration as I am. I felt like a helpless toy of nature. A far-fetched notion – after all, I have the strength, technique and speed of reaction to overcome gravity, though only up to a point – we are too perilously close to being stripped off like drops of water. Perhaps it is the fear of paralysing safety and humdrum routine of everyday existence that makes me break out and challenge nature, risking everything.

A small twig broke off, fell down and splashed in a puddle, disturbing the mirror surface. In some way I see myself within my sport reflected in such a mirror; a fleeting vision which may be shattered at any time. What fear I experienced before I reached the first ring bolt! If a tiny sandstone hold had crumbled I would have been unable to avoid a horrific fall – all the way to the ground. Of course afterwards on the summit the sense of fear added to the sense of joy and achievement. But this did not last for long – as soon as I reached the top I was already thinking of the next route. I was not going to rest on my laurels – I am far too young for that.

It was a make-believe landscape reminiscent of childhood fairy-tales read by my grandmother. A world of myth and legend out of which a unicorn or giant could have suddenly materialised. Towers of rock appeared from nothingness and disappeared just as mysteriously – a constantly changing spectre. I began to understand the fascination it held for the local climbers, to understand their attachment to the land – a necessity if they are not to feel trapped and isolated. The local climbers spend all their

time here in their own back yard and they are the masters. Unfortunately few of them have a chance to use their skills elsewhere. Only on the vertical walls are there no political fences. They know that free-climbing evolved here and has been going on for some eighty years. From these crags and rock towers the sport of free-climbing has spread all over the world.

Rathen, Elbsandstein

Eiszeit, Xa
Dreifingerturm

I feel I have only a certain degree of control and, like
a drop of water, my link with the cliff seems fragile
– I am a mere plaything of nature.

Grünes Ungeheuer, IXc
Heringstein

Teufelsturm, Ostseite

Teufelsturm,
Schmilka

Pferdefuß, X a
Teufelsturm

Osternest, VIIIb
Heringstein

Pferdefuß, Xa
Teufelsturm

Jo Jo Variante, IXb
Heringstein

Direkte Südkante, VIIc
N. Pfaffenschluchtspitze

Engelsflügel, IXb (2nd Asc.)
Doppelturm

Engelsflügel

W. GERMANY

When I began climbing at the age of fifteen I already had a long learning period behind me. Even before I could walk I was humped on my father's shoulders for weekend trips through our home mountains, often visiting areas in which I would later climb. Right from the start I felt at home in the world of mountains and nature, an attraction which has become stronger with the passage of time.

Initially I could only look and wonder at the climbers I spied from the paths, but I was fascinated by their activities. Later, when I eventually persuaded my parents to allow me to try my hand at climbing, there was no holding me back. I spent every free moment on the practise crags just ten minutes' cycle-ride from our house. I soon became obsessed with climbing, which did not entirely please my poor parents and long-suffering teachers at a time when I should have been studying for my exams.

At first my climbing ambitions were to tackle the great mountain faces of the Alps, the Dolomites, the Kaisergebirge and the Wetterstein. Although the "Sport Climbing Movement" had already started in Germany I knew little about it. It was only when I saw pictures of rock-climbing in the Pfalz and Frankenjura that I realised that this was my destiny – climbing difficult rock faces rather than the great mountains. I had a lot to learn and a long way to go but I imitated my heroes and began an intensive training programme through which I discovered my true potential.

The low hills and lesser mountains of the Frankenjura, Altmühltal and Pfalz now became my second home. At first I was only interested in the most difficult routes – the harder and steeper they were, the more I liked them. The charm of the half-timbered houses, the romantic crag-top castles, not to mention the pleasures of the beer gardens, were entirely lost on me. Such was my dedication that even the celebrated giant slabs of Apfelkuchen (applecake) available at the Kroderwirt could not keep me away from an unclimbed chunk of rock.

I have mellowed with the passage of time and have become a little less frantic in pursuit of my obsession, though I have lost none of the ambition which is so essential to any serious athlete. Today my perspective has broadened and I realise that there is more to climbing than just knocking off the hardest and most famous routes and I am now much more receptive to the

whole range of experiences which our sport has to offer.

As I have become more sensitive to my surroundings I have become increasingly aware of some of the environmental damage caused by climbers. As "Sport Climbing" has become more popular, so the problems have increased, to the extent that conservationists are now pressing for the closure of several important crags. One such example is the Schelleneckpfeiler in the Altmühltal, famous in West Germany as the scene of the first Grade 10 climb, established in 1985 by Jerry Moffat. Many leading climbers seem to think that they have a God-given right to deface and pollute the crags. In the Frankenjura they are even prepared to cheat themselves and future generations by chopping out holds and threads in their lust for new climbs.

The future of climbing lies in our own hands and it hurts me a lot to have to point out how, in my own area, many climbers are so uncaring with their priceless commodity – the rock. If at some future time we are restricted to climbing on artificial walls inside sports halls it will be our own fault. By the time that happens I will have long quit the sport I love.

Sitting in the Barenbrunner Hof in the Pfalz in front of a steaming Zwiebelkuchen (onion cake) and a glass of foaming Federweissem (local beer), fingers throbbing after a hard and exhilarating day's climbing, it is easy to forget these depressing thoughts. Just like generations

of climbers before us we enjoy meeting in the convivial atmosphere of the Bierhaus to talk excitedly about our climbing. The stories of heroic deeds will always be the same, only the climbers change.

That's what it used to be like, that's how it is today, and that's how it will be in the future. Or will it?

The Face, X- (2nd Asc.)
Altmühltal

The Face, X-
Altmühltal

Today I see climbing from a different standpoint
– I understand that it is much more than just
doing the hardest routes.

Erdnußflip, X- (1st Asc.)
Oberau

Kraftmaschine, IX- (1st Asc.)
Oberau

Elektrischer Sturm, IX+
N. Frankenjura

Amadeus Schwarzenegger, X-
N. Frankenjura

Rote Wand, VIII
Südpfalz

Magnetfinger, IX-
Südpfalz

France 6
England (and Wales) 28
USA 46
Japan 74
Australia 94
East Germany 114
West Germany 130

UIAA Scale	France	USA	England		Australia	GDR
VI +	6 a	5.10 a	5 b	E 2	19	VII c
VII −	6 b	5.10 b			20	VIII a
VII		5.10 c	5 c		21	VIII b
VII +	6 c	5.10 d		E 3		VIII c
		5.11 a			22	
VIII −	7 a	5.11 b	6 a		23	IX a
VIII		5.11 c		E 4	24	IX b
		5.11 d			25	IX c
VIII +	7 b	5.12 a	6 b		26	X a
		5.12 b		E 5		
IX −	7 c	5.12 c			27	
IX		5.12 d	6 c		28	
		5.13 a		E 6	29	X b
IX +	8 a	5.13 b				
X −		5.13 c	7 a		30	
		5.13 d			31	
X	8 b	5.14 a		E 7	32	X c
X +		5.14 b	7 b			
XI −	8 c	5.14 c			33	